FREE SAMPLE — PLEASE EXAMINE
Not for Sale   Do Not Sell!
We Welcome Your Order!
To Order, Please Call (585) 586-9191

To Arabel,

Kindest wishes.

Halif Rogers

9/07/2013

What Must I Do To Be Saved?

Dr. Habib J. Khoury, B.A., M.A., M.Div., Th.D.
Founding President & CEO
Biblical Counselor / Author / Theologian
Baptist **A**rabic **M**inistries **I**ncorporated
Biblical **C**ounseling & Literature **C**enter ™

BAMI Publications ™
Fairport, New York 14450-0485

What Must I Do To Be Saved?

COPYRIGHT © 2010
BY
DR. HABIB J. KHOURY, TH.D.

No part of this publication may be reproduced,
Stored in a retrieval system,
Or transmitted in any form or by any means,
Electronic, mechanical, photocopying, recording, or otherwise,
Without the written permission of the copyright owner.

First Printing — November 2010 — 20,500
Second Printing — January 2011 — 20,500

Booklet #1 — Published by
BAMI PUBLICATIONS™
POST OFFICE BOX 485
FAIRPORT, NEW YORK 14450-0485
www.bamipublications.com

All Scripture is taken from the NEW AMERICAN STANDARD
BIBLE, copyright 1960, 1962, 1963, 1968, 1971, 1972,
1973, 1975, 1977, 1995 by The Lockman Foundation.
Used by permission.

All illustration photos are obtained from the public domain.
Photo from Space is courtesy of NASA.

ISBN 10/13 — 0-9829843-1-6 / 978-0-9829843-1-4

Library of Congress Control Number: **2010912901**

ISTC A03-2010-000000CD-5

Printed in the Beautiful United States of America.

Table of Contents

The Urgency for Salvation	7
The Nature of Sin in God's Sight	12
Salvation's Prerequisites	17
The Meaning of Repentance from Sin	19
The Meaning of Saving Faith in Jesus Christ	21
The Lord God Grants to the Sinner His Prerequisites for Salvation	23
Your Regeneration Is Instantaneous!	25
Your Regeneration Is Non-Repetitious!	27
Your Steps to Receive Christ the Savior & Lord	28
The Assurance of Your Salvation	32
Confess Your Faith in Christ Publicly	34
The Holy Spirit Now Begins His Work of Sanctification!	37
Your Regeneration Is Irreversible!	40
The Bible Evidence of Genuine Salvation	42
Follow the Lord Jesus in Believer's Baptism	44
Join a New Testament Church Immediately	45
Your Required Christian Giving	48

Consider this Vital Truth	49
I Am Available to Assist You	50
Use this Booklet as a Tool for Evangelism	52
References Made in the Text	53

The New Testament question, *"Sirs, what must I do to be saved?"* [1] is the most crucial question a human being can ask. Its answer can transform one from being a slave to sin, to becoming a slave to righteousness. Its answer can regenerate a self-centered life into a Christ-centered life. Indeed, its answer can change a man's purpose and direction in life. It can grant the forgiveness of sins and eternal life to the sinner condemned by God to eternal damnation. This was the ancient question asked by a jailer of Philippi. [2] It was directed to the Apostle Paul and to his companion Silas, some two thousand years ago: *"Sirs, what must I do to be saved?"*

The Divinely-inspired answer from the Apostle and his companion came simple and clear: *"Believe in the Lord Jesus, and you will be saved, you and your household."* [3] Faith in the Lord Jesus Christ is the channel through which God's Grace communicates salvation to the human soul. This so-great a salvation is offered to YOU right now, and is available to your entire family as well. *"As for God, His way is blameless; the word of the Lord is tried* [tested & proven true & reliable]*; He is a shield to all who take refuge in Him."* [4] **Give your most serious thinking to the most important matter in your life — your eternal salvation!** *"For what does it profit a man to gain the whole world, and forfeit his* [own] *soul?"* (Mark 8:36).

THE URGENCY FOR YOUR SALVATION

All human beings in God's sight are declared sick, [5] lost, [6] and dead [7] in trespasses and sins. The Divine **guilty** verdict is universal: *"for all have sinned and fall short of the glory of God."* [8] All people [9] on earth do sin, all have sinned, [10] all are children under God's wrath, [11] all are sinners estranged from God, [12] all are corrupt and deceitful in nature, [13] all are antagonistic to God, [14] all are identified with God's Adversary, [15] all possess death-doomed sin-weakened bodies, [16] all are debased in character and conduct, [17] and all are enslaved to personal sin.[18] Indeed, with King David of old, one can utter a deep sigh of anguish: *"Help, LORD, for the godly man ceases to be, for the faithful disappear from among the sons of men."* [19] **Your salvation is urgent, having the sense of a pressing importance!**

Concurrently, **man in his sin** is ugly and contemptible in God's sight. The Lord God likens the sinner to the lower class of creatures that take things as they come, [20] and do not discern the working of the arm of the Lord. [21] Assuredly, *"All of us growl like bears, and moan sadly like doves; we hope for justice, but there is none, for salvation, but it is far from us."* [22] Indeed**,** Our tragic and consequential depravity is seen in the revealing words of Prophet Isaiah, *"your iniquities have made a separation between you and your God, and your sins have hidden His face from you so that He does not hear."* [23] The Lord Jesus Christ was persecuted by the Pharisees of His days who were lovers of money. While scoffing at Him, He said to them what applies to us today: *"You are those who justify yourselves in the sight of men, but God knows your hearts; for that which is highly esteemed among men is detestable in the sight of God."* [24] **Your salvation is urgent, demanding immediate attention!**

Man is in bondage to his many sins.

Consequently, *"The way of the Lord is a stronghold to the upright, but ruin to the workers of iniquity."* [25] Each sin is said to have its inescapable ultimate wages from the Lord God: *"the wages of sin is death."* [26] Each of our sins is eternally fatal! This is a most sobering thought in light of the fact that *"God seeks what has passed by."* [27] He keeps records of each and all of our sins and holds us accountable for each and all of them.

Each day, the accumulation of the wages of our sins is on an alarming increase.

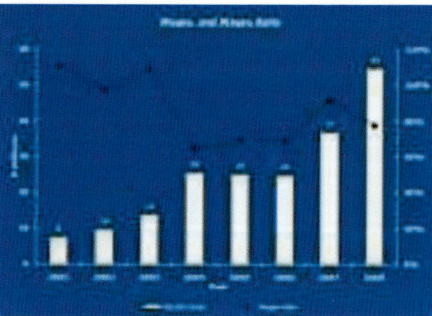

YOU ARE ON A HIGH-SPEED TRAIN MOVING TOWARD ETERNAL DESTRUCTION – – GET OFF NOW!

Thus, given the fact that *"it is appointed for men to die once and after this comes judgment,"* [28] it is most urgent indeed that we receive the eternal salvation of our souls. **Your salvation is urgent, pressing upon you to take immediate action!**

In addition, the **Divine law of sowing and reaping** in the spiritual realm is very depressive indeed: *"Do not be deceived, God is not mocked; for whatever a man sows, this he will also reap."* [29] Such a Divinely-appointed law fosters extreme pessimism for every one of us sinners. For if man must reap inevitably the evil that he sows, then his end assuredly will be destruction. Indeed, each human sin produces continuing and cumulative effects. Each evil act, conscious or unconscious, brings in its wake misery and bondage to man. Seeking to escape the consequences of his own deeds, the sinner becomes involved in other evils which further complicate his fate. Therefore, only the interposition of the supernatural power of The Risen Jesus Christ, to arrest the downward trend of man, can bring about a permanent deliverance for man. **Your salvation is urgent, calling upon you to acknowledge your sinful condition!**

Furthermore, **the complete dependency of the spiritual dimension of man** upon the Word of God demands the immediate salvation of man. The Lord God created man's body utterly dependent upon **physical food**, and He created our spirits completely dependent upon **spiritual food**. Indeed, the Lord Jesus so asserted: *"Man shall not live on bread alone, but on every word that proceeds out of the mouth of God."* (Matthew 4:4). Thus, man without the Bible is a *tragic failure* in God's sight. Even the prayer of such a person is rejected by the Lord God: *"He who turns away his ear from listening to the law, even his prayer is an abomination."* (Proverbs 28:9). Indeed, *"If I regard wickedness in my heart, the Lord will not hear."* (Psalms 66:18).

Man is created utterly dependent on the Word of God.

However, being spiritually dead in trespasses and sins, man has no appetite for the Word of God. His sinful condition drives him away from feeding on the Word of God. Therefore, he urgently needs an immediate salvation which would create in him and would trigger within him a genuine appetite for daily feeding on the Word of God, the Holy Scriptures. **Your salvation is urgent, calling upon you to turn to God's Word!**

Moreover, the urgency for **YOUR** personal salvation is further stated in the words of **the Lord Jesus Christ demanding the supernatural regeneration of the sinner**: *"Truly, truly, I say to you, unless one is born again* [from above] *he cannot see the kingdom of God."* [30] and *"Do not be amazed that I said to you, <u>You must be born again</u>* [from above]*."* (John 3:7). **TO BE SAVED, YOU MUST EXPERIENCE THE NEW BIRTH; YOU MUST BE BORN AGAIN! Every one of us desperately and urgently needs a**

permanent and a Made-in-Heaven change from within! Your salvation is urgent, demanding that you come to the Savior!

Nevertheless, many of today's millions who claim to be born-again, **NEVER** indeed have been saved. Their lifestyles tell on them (read: I John 2:3-6). They **NEVER** had a genuine experience of the New Birth demanded by the Lord God, which new birth produces a lifestyle full of righteousness and obedience to God: *"Since you have in obedience to the truth purified your souls for a sincere love of the brethren, fervently love one another from the heart, for you have been born again not of seed which is perishable but imperishable, that is, through the living and enduring word of God...the word of the Lord endures forever."* (I Peter 1:22-25). **Your salvation is urgent, necessitating that you must experience the New Birth!**

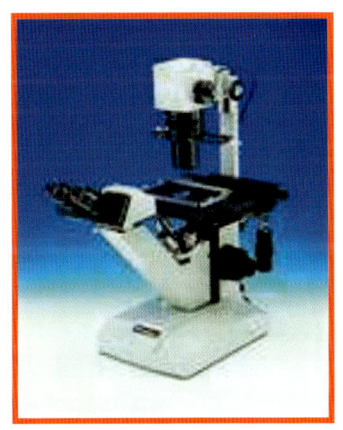

Examine yourself like under a high-power microscope.

An often-widely-quoted Socratic injunction says: *"the unexamined life is not worth living."* For a quality life worth living, indeed, YOU MUST PERIODICALLY AND REPEATEDLY EXAMINE YOUR OWN LIFE! Yes, indeed, examining yourself under the light of God's moral standards is demanded by the Lord God Himself: *"Test yourselves to see if you are in the faith; examine yourselves!"* [85] Like King David of old, you must pray, *"Examine me, O Lord, and try me; test my mind and my heart."* [86] Here, in this Booklet, is YOUR **golden opportunity** to examine your own life under the shining light of God's revealed Word, the infallible Bible. God's Word is living and active, and the Lord God uses His Word to reveal to us the truth about ourselves and others, and to transform individuals in a marvelous and profound manner that only the Lord God Himself can achieve. Do you want Him to regenerate **YOU** today? Please read on carefully and thoughtfully. **Your salvation is urgent — you must surrender to God's work of regeneration!**

THE NATURE OF SIN IN GOD'S SIGHT

Every person seems to have his own list of what is sin and of what is not sin. Some even have adopted the extreme position of denying the existence of moral absolutes binding on the entire human race. However, from God's perspective — *the only perspective that really and ultimately matters* — the term **sin** covers a wide range of human failures. Indeed, His moral standards, to which He expects every one of us to measure up, are far above and beyond our own standards.

Yes, indeed, the Lord God demands that all His children would mimic Him,[33] **striving toward doctrinal,**[34] **moral and ethical purity.**[35] He abhors each form and all forms of evil. He is the Holy God of Abraham, Isaac and Jacob, the Father of our Lord Jesus Christ. Therefore, in the Christian Bible man's **sin** is portrayed primarily **an act against the Holy God Himself**. It violates His Person, it undermines His moral character, and it defies His Laws. *Negatively,* **sin** **denies that which is true of God**. *Positively,* **sin** **is an active opposition to God**.

In reality, God's perfect Nature is the Standard for Universal Morality: *"Therefore you are to be perfect as your heavenly Father is perfect."* [36] He Himself is the Source and the Embodiment of MORALITY (the absolute standard of what is right and good), and He expects the entire world to abide by His revealed Standard! Thus, **sin** **is anything unlike God**, an active moral evil that resides in the center of man's life and personality. In fact, **sin** **is man's refusal to hold God and His revealed will (the Holy Scriptures) as the center and the sphere of his own daily lifestyle**. It includes the liability to punishment from God and the corruption of the human nature. **Sin** grieves our loving Father; it provokes God to anger; and it brings God's judgment upon the sinner.

Furthermore, **sin** destroys the ability of the human soul to recognize its own sinfulness. Hence, the destructive popular assertion — I am OK, you are OK — ignoring and denying the pressing need for self-examination and supernatural regeneration.

However, the faithful and clear proclamation of the written

> *"Your word I have treasured in my heart, That I may not sin against You."* Psalms 119:11.

Word of God, the whole Counsel of God, brings an awakening to the human soul. Self-examination brings chastisement and saves the soul from a sleeping sickness; and the sincere and earnest confession of **sin** to God, through the Lord Jesus Christ, brings the soul to a state of healing and healthy satisfaction.

Correspondingly, **sin** is missing the mark of God's Moral Standard;[37] it is a deviation or a falling aside from God's lofty requirements;[38] and it is a making crooked that which is right in God's sight.[39] Indeed, **sin** is a rebellion against the Lord God,[40] a betrayal of a trust,[41] an offense, an error, a negligence,[42] an evil principle within the nature of man,[43] creating a bent or a bias toward disobedience to God and toward wickedness.[44]

Accordingly, reading the New Testament would provide many insights into the high moral standards that the Lord God demands from mankind. As noted above, these moral standards spring out of God's own moral perfections, and His moral laws are the demands of His moral perfections from His rational creatures. For four lists of specific sins named in the New Testament, read: Revelation 21:8; II Timothy 3:1-5; I Corinthians 6:9, 10; and Galatians 5:19-21.

In addition, other numerous specific sins are named in the Bible, covering every human failure. Some examples include, but are not limited to the following: **A lack of tongue control** is **sin** (James 1:26; 3:1-12); the mere entertainment of **a foolish thought** is sin (Proverbs 24:9); **consulting any witch, fortuneteller, or a psychic**, is an abomination to the Lord God (I Samuel 15:23; Deuteronomy 18:9-13); **falling short of loving *"your neighbor as yourself"*** will be accounted for (Romans 13:8-10); a lack of generosity (II Corinthians 8:2, 3; Proverbs 23:6-8) or **a poor hospitality** is **sin** (Romans 12:13; I Timothy 3:2; Titus 1:8; I Peter 4:9). Not to do your very best at the job is sin (Ephesians 6:5; Proverbs 10:4, 5). Not to deal fairly with your employees is sin (Ephesians 6:9; James 5:4).

Similarly, **bribery** is sin (Exodus 23:8; Deuteronomy 16:19; Proverbs 15:27; 29:4), and so is **dishonesty** (II Corinthians 4:2; Proverbs 21:8; 20:23). An **outburst of anger** is sin (Ephesians 4:31; Colossians 3:8; cf. Matthew 5:21-24). Also, **envy**, **malice**, **jealousy**, **hatred**, **boasting**, a lack of discernment, **a lack of trustworthiness**, backbiting, **strife**, violence, **deceit**, **gluttony** and **greed** are sins (Romans 1:29-32; Proverbs 28:7). *Sex outside the husband-wife relationship* is **sin** (Matthew 15:16-20; I Corinthians 6:13, 18; 10:8; cf. Numbers 25:1-8; I Thessalonians 4:1-8; Exodus 20:14). **Lust** (Matthew 5:27-28; 6:22)**, lying** (Colossians 3:8-9; Philippians 4:8-9; Revelation 21:8; cf. Proverbs 12:22; 21:6; Psalms 119:163), stealing (I Corinthians 6:10; cf. Exodus 20:15), **murder** (Exodus 20:13), **gossip** (Leviticus 19:16), **a lack of faith in God** (I Timothy 1:19; Hebrews 10:38; 11:6), a disobedience to parents (Exodus 20:12; Ephesians 6:1-3; Proverbs 30:17), **a wife's disobedience to her husband** (Ephesians 5:22-24; I Peter 3:1-6), **a rush to judgment** (John 7:24), and **a self-absorbing love of material things, selfish ambitions** (I John 2:16; cf. Matthew 6:22-24) — each is a **sin** repeatedly condemned by the Lord God.

Likewise, **a false teaching**, one not in harmony with the teachings of the Written Word of God, is **sin** (Matthew 15:8-9; Galatians 1:8; II Peter 2:1-22). **Not reading God's Written Word** regularly is **sin** (Proverbs 28:9; Psalms 1:2; 119:1, 51, 53, 92, 97; Colossians 3:16).

Failing to participate in the proclamation of the Whole Counsel of God is **sin** (I Corinthians 9:16; Matthew 28:19-20). **Withholding the Lord's tithes** is **sin** (Malachi 3:8-12). Obviously, these are widely-spread sins, to the extent that everyone is guilty of at least several of them, if not all of them. Indeed, the short-term present belongs to Satan and his servants, but **the eternal future belongs to Christ the King and His followers!**

The Bible's lists of named sins go on and on. Each human sin, however, has *death* [45] for its wages: [46] *"For the wages of sin is death, but the free gift of God is eternal life in Christ Jesus our Lord."* Indeed, the Lord God has given us His commandments so *"that we should keep them diligently."* [47] Our Lord's verdict is clear: *"If you love Me, you will keep my commandments."* [48] Any deliberate disobedience to God's Word is evidence of a lack of love toward God. Nevertheless, we MUST love God above all other love: *"You shall love the Lord your God with all your heart, and with all your soul, and with all your mind."* [49] Certainly, our sinfulness is beyond all human measure! Nevertheless, a radical change from within the individual is definitely possible and certain, through the Lord Jesus Christ!

When the first human father, Adam, chose deliberately to commit that first sin, his connection with God was shot off, and his spirit, soul and body tumbled instantaneously into the realm of spiritual, physical and everlasting death (Genesis 2:17; 3:8). Indeed, Adam and Eve, having become the First Parents of all sinners, were expelled out of the Garden of God's perfections. They went out covered with fear and shame.

"But may it never be that I would boast, except in the cross of our Lord Jesus Christ." Galatians 6:14.

However, the Lord God, because of His infinite love and through the promised Savior (Genesis 3:15), [i] put them on the way to become infinitely grander and nobler than they ever were after their fall. They were saved by faith in the promised Savior to come, restoring onto them the perfect **Image of God** in which they were originally created, and which **Image of God** they had distorted by sinning.

Likewise, the Lord God wants to do in YOU a similar saving work, a wonderful and a radical makeover, a supernatural transformation for the world to behold and to marvel at. He wants to transform YOU onto the glorious character likeness of His Son Jesus Christ!

Because the Holy God cannot accept a condemned sinner in His pure and eternal Heaven; and because the sinner is condemned by God to death; motivated by His own infinite love, the Lord God sent His Son Jesus Christ, the promised Messiah Savior, to die on behalf of every sinner, including YOU! The eternal goal of this Divine Redemption is that the Lord God would be glorified through the marvelous transformation of the sinner. His righteousness will be manifested through the sinner's spiritual freedom from his own bondage to sin, and through the sinner's adoption of a new life of righteousness (Bible: the process of *sanctification*). In addition, God's eternal love and justice are satisfied through the eternal salvation (Bible: the act of *glorification*) of the sinner into the glories of God's Heaven.

Indeed, through the identification of the sinless Jesus Christ with human sin, on a cross, and through His bodily resurrection victorious over sin, death and Hades, we now can be brought back into perfect harmony with God. Therefore, *"He who believes in the Son has eternal life; but he who does not obey the Son will not see life, but the wrath* [judgment] *of God abides on him."* [50]

---

[i] The promise of Gen. 3:15 is recognized by many theologians as the *Protoevangelium*, the First Gospel. This is the first proclamation of the Gospel of Jesus Christ, and it was made by the Lord God Himself, to Adam and Eve. The Gospel of Jesus Christ, however, shines most brightly in the New Testament where the record of the fulfillment of this Divine promise is preserved, interpreted, proclaimed, defended and embraced.

SALVATION'S PREREQUISITES

The God-breathed [51] Holy Scriptures assure us repeatedly that the Lord God takes no pleasure in the eternal condemnation of sinners: *"As I live, declares the Lord GOD, I take no pleasure in the death of the wicked, but rather that the wicked turn from his way* [repent] *and live."* [52]

Most assuredly, the Lord God fully desires that all men and all women would be saved, coming to the knowledge of the truth which is in the Lord Jesus Christ: *"This is good and acceptable in the sight of God our Savior, who desires all men to be saved and to come to the knowledge of the truth."* [53] While His holy desire is that all would be saved, He allows His rational creatures to make their own choices, not coerced by Him. [54]

God's Two Prerequisites for Your Salvation:
1. Repent from your sins; and,
2. Believe in the Lord Jesus Christ.

However, it is our Lord's command that repentance for forgiveness of sins would be preached to all: *"and that repentance for forgiveness of sins would be proclaimed in His name to all the nations, beginning from Jerusalem."* [55] Likewise, faith in the Lord Jesus Christ grants eternal life to the believer: *"so that whoever believes will in Him* [the Lord Jesus Christ] *have eternal life."* [56]

Indeed, our loving Heavenly Father is not wishing for any sinner to perish; but that all people everywhere should come at once to **a genuine repentance from sin**,[57] and to **a saving faith in His Son Jesus Christ**.[58] These are His two prerequisites for the salvation of the sinner.

The Lord Jesus Christ's preaching in Galilee: *"repent and believe in the gospel,"* [59] and the Apostle Paul's declaration to all *"that they should repent and turn to God,"* [60] each speaks of God's two prerequisites for man's salvation: **repentance from sin** and **saving faith in the Lord Jesus Christ** as the Savior and Lord of life. Indeed, the Lord God demands that you would *earnestly denounce the life of sin you have been living*, and that you would *sincerely commit yourself to follow the Lord Jesus Christ for the rest of your life on earth*.

Accordingly, **repentance from sin** and **saving faith in the Lord Jesus** go hand in hand; you cannot have one without the other. Both are God's gift to the sinner seeking salvation. They are His must-have prerequisites, for Him to perform the Divine surgical work of *regeneration* upon the condemned sinner. Yes, **they are God's two prerequisites for your own eternal salvation**. No one was ever saved, and no one can ever be saved, without meeting these two prerequisites established by the Lord God. Indeed, without **repentance from sin**,[61] there is **no** forgiveness of sins; and without **faith in the Lord Jesus Christ**,[62] no one can please the Lord God and no one can earn eternal life. The Lord the Holy Spirit gives both of them, faith and repentance, to the sinner sincerely and earnestly seeking his own salvation.

However, the alternative to salvation is living under the wrath of God in this life and in the life to come: *"He who believes in Him* [the Lord Jesus Christ] *is not judged; he who does not believe has been judged already, because he has not believed in the name of the only begotten Son of God."* [63] (See Endnote 108 on the everlasting **Lake of Fire**).

My Dear Reader: Do you sincerely want the Lord God's forgiveness of your sins, and do you desire a new life pleasing to the Lord God? I sincerely hope that you do! I earnestly pray that you do! I have invested my entire life (now more than 55 years) into bringing the message of this blessed hope to people like you! Nothing would make me happier than learning of your genuine salvation!

THE MEANING OF REPENTANCE FROM SIN

The inerrant Christian Holy Scriptures inspired by the Lord God represent **repentance from sin** as essentially a change of view with regard to sin, to God, to the Bible, and to one's own self. [ii] This means that the sinner, forsaking all previously held views related to these major subjects, adopts for himself *God's own view* of God and His world, as revealed in the Christian Holy Bible. Yes, the sinner adopts the Christian Bible's view of the world. Whatever the Bible says is so.

> **Building your life on the teachings and the principles of the infallible Bible – is like building a house on solid rock.**

In addition, one's **Repentance from sin** involves a profound sorrow for his sin: *"For the sorrow that is according to the will of God produces a repentance without regret* [for repentance]*, leading to salvation, but the sorrow of the world produces death."* [64]

[ii] The observance of religious rites or the leading of an ascetic lifestyle does not constitute an evidence of genuine repentance. Likewise, the Roman Catholic *penance* must not be equated with **repentance**. *Penance* consists of specific acts prescribed by the Catholic priest presumably to help pay for the temporal punishment of sin, whereby shortening one's supposed stay in purgatory. *Penance* is neither required by God nor is it an act toward God. It is simply an act toward the Catholic Church, becoming the meritorious grounds for the Roman Church's pardon. **True repentance**, however, entails a radical change of mind, desire, and intent regarding one's sinful condition, producing a new lifestyle of obedience to God's Word. Such **repentance** is initiated by the Lord God with the full participation of the sinner. Unlike the sorrow of the world (2 Corinthians 7:10), which leads only to feelings of guilt, shame, despair, self-pity and depression — **true repentance** is arrived at by a genuine sorrow over one's own sins, accompanied by a sincere desire to turn away from such sins, a genuine desire for God's pardon, and a determination to submit to the Will of God.

Repentance from sin also includes a genuine desire to be freed fully from the life of sin, and a sincere heartfelt desire for God's pardon. [65] Furthermore, because the fundamental nature of human *sin* is to *act independent of God*, **repentance from sin** includes one's *determination* to submit to the Will of God. Thus, **anything unlike the Lord God (as revealed in the Bible) is sin**. Therefore, in repentance, the sinner's general heart's attitude *becomes* a genuine commitment to obey the will of God as revealed in the Holy Scriptures.

Likewise, as it was in the case of a well-known repentant chief tax collector named Zaccheus in the New Testament, [66] **repentance from sin** includes a specific and a generous *restitution* to the object(s) of sin. **Zaccheus said:** *"Behold, Lord, half of my possessions I will give to the poor, and if I have defrauded anyone of anything, I will give back four times as much."* [67] **The Lord Jesus Replied:** *"Today salvation has come to this house...for the Son of Man has come to seek and to save that which was lost"* [68] The sinner compensates to the one or to the people he sinned against.

Thus, in light of the fact that *"God seeks what has passed by,"* [69] *restitution* is an essential component of **repentance from sin**: *"Therefore repent and return, so that your sins may be wiped away, in order that times of refreshing may come from the presence of the Lord."* [70]

Accordingly, a genuine **repentance from sin** includes each and all of the following: the sinner's adoption of the Bible's world view, the sinner's profound sorrow for sin, the sinner's sincere desire to be freed fully from the life of sin, the sinner's heartfelt desire for God's pardon, the sinner's determination to submit to the Will of God, and the sinner's generous restitution to the object(s) of sin. [71]

My Dear Reader, examine yourself: Do you have a profound sorrow for your sins? Do you possess a sincere desire to forsake all sin? Do you *really* want to be freed from your bondage to sin? Do you now hunger for God's pardon? Are you determined from now on, to submit to the Will of God? Are you willing to make a generous restitution to all against whom you have sinned?

THE MEANING OF SAVING FAITH IN JESUS CHRIST

Faith in the Lord Jesus Christ, as *the channel* of God's saving grace to the human soul, is far more than the mere mental assent to the Biblical assertions about God and His Christ. A sheer mental assent to the facts of Scripture, though a first step toward saving faith, is by itself incapable of producing a life of obedience to God, and is ascribed to the evil demons as their kind of faith: *"You believe that God is one. You do well; the demons also believe, and shudder."* [72]

Biblically, **saving faith in Christ** is the total surrender of the self to the Savior, to Him who will do the full and complete work of salvation upon the sinner. It is that radical decision of one's own will to turn from the self and to deliver himself totally to the Savior. It is a sincere faith in the Savior similar to the faith of a young child thrusting himself fully, with great confidence, into the open arms of his loving Daddy: *"Truly, I say to you, whoever does not receive the Kingdom of God like a child will not enter it at all."* [73]

Thus, **saving faith in Jesus Christ** is a childlike faith which receives salvation from God with the humility and the meekness of a child, and with the willingness to submit fully to Christ's supreme authority. This **saving faith** in the Lord Jesus Christ brings about a change of purpose and a change of direction in the believing sinner. Like a patient lying at the surgical table, surrendering to the skilled work of his surgeon, the sinner lies before the Divine Surgeon, seeking his own eternal healing as the outcome guaranteed by the Lord God. [iii]

[iii] According to the Bible, there is no salvation for the sinner apart from the personal application of the Death and the Resurrection of the Lord Jesus Christ. He alone is *"the Lamb of God who takes away the sin of the world."* (John 1:29). He is the **Mercy Seat** for sinful man constantly standing before the justifiably angry God. When sin is removed, God's wrath against that sin is appeased or satisfied. The Lord Jesus Christ died instead of and for the benefit of the sinner. Likewise, His resurrection is a new redemptive act with a universal import: *"I am the resurrection and the life; He who believes in Me will live even if he dies."* (John 11:25). Faith in the Lord Jesus Christ, as the channel of God's saving grace to the human soul, is far more than the mere intellectual assent to Bible facts about God and His Christ. A faith in God that does not produce a lifestyle obedient to God is ascribed to evil and vile spirits: *"the demons also believe, and shudder."* (James 2:19), and brings no salvation to the sinner. **Saving faith**, however, is the total surrender of the self to the Savior.

From God's own perspective, this means that **a life of righteousness** is *the natural fruit or product* of a genuine experience of salvation. Those who were all their lives *"slaves of sin,"* upon receiving the Savior by faith, were *"freed from sin,"* and now they *"became slaves of righteousness."* [74] The sinner surrenders to Christ, receives Christ the Savior and Lord; but God the Almighty does all the saving in and for the sinner! The immediate outcome of this faith in Jesus Christ is perfect **peace with God**: *"Therefore, having been justified* [declared, not guilty!] *by faith, we have peace with God through our Lord Jesus Christ."* [75] When the sinner obtains peace with God, then it becomes possible for him to develop peace with himself and with others.

STEPS TO FAITH IN GOD:
NO FAITH
TO
    LITTLE FAITH
TO
        GREAT FAITH

In addition, *the content* of **saving faith in Jesus Christ** includes the sinner's own persuasion that the Lord God has appointed the Lord Jesus Christ as the only way to God the Father, the only Savior of the world: *"And there is salvation in no one else* [other than Jesus Christ], *for there is no other name under heaven that has been given among men by which we must be saved."* [76] Thus, the believing sinner sincerely subscribes to the historically common Christian confession that: [77]

Great is the mystery of godliness:
He was revealed in the flesh,
Was vindicated in the Spirit,
Seen by angels,
Proclaimed among the nations,
Believed in the world,
Taken up in glory.

Conclusively, saving faith in the Lord Jesus Christ is the radical surrender of one's own will to the Savior, the reception of God's salvation with humility and meekness, and the adoption of the Bible and its teachings as God's infallible Word for all mankind.

My Dear Reader, are you willing to surrender yourself to the Savior, saying, *"Your Will, not my will, be done in my life?"* Do you indeed recognize yourself unworthy of God's gift of salvation? Do you believe the Bible is God's infallible Word for all mankind? Do you recognize the Bible as God's Word to you personally?

THE LORD GOD GRANTS TO THE SINNER HIS PREREQUISITES FOR SALVATION

A sinner condemned by the Almighty is utterly incapable of earning his own way to Heaven. Otherwise, there would have been no need for the coming of the Lord Jesus to earth. Indeed, apart from the redemptive work of the Savior Lord (His substitutionary death, resurrection and intercession on behalf of sinners), there is no single act or any series of good acts, which you possibly can perform for gaining God's acceptance. Yes, you cannot do anything for the purpose of earning the forgiveness of your countless sins abhorred by the Lord God! Absolutely, none! Absolutely, not!

Due to the fact that ours is a sinful human nature condemned by the Lord God, no human merits, no talents and gifts, no successes and achievements, and no material wealth and human refinement can score points with the Most High God! The Lord God cannot be impressed by any one of us individually, or by any number of us collectively. **In His holy sight, all of us are sick, lost, dead, rejected, and condemned sinners!** Indeed, our sinful nature alienates us totally from any approval, fellowship or acceptance with the Omniscient and Holy God. His holy and pure Nature is described by an ancient prophet in this manner: *"Your eyes are too pure to approve evil, and You cannot look on wickedness* *with favor."* [78] Yes, indeed, in the words of Prophet Isaiah, this sad fact of separation from God is emphasized: *"But your iniquities* [built-in sinful nature & grossly immoral acts] *have made a separation between you and your God, and your sins* [see the nature of sin above] *have hidden His face from you so that He does not hear."* [79]

Accordingly, sinful man, unaided by Divine Grace, is of himself incapable of turning to God, unable to repent from sin, and is clueless about exercising saving faith in the Wonderful Savior. The Lord Jesus asserted: *"No one can come to Me unless the Father who sent Me draws him; and I will raise him up on the last day."* [80] Indeed, no one can live a life of righteousness prior to receiving salvation. Salvation is a free gift received by the sinner; **not** a reward earned.

To the contrary, sin destroys the ability of the human soul to recognize its own sinfulness. However, the proclamation of God's Word brings an awakening to the soul. Self-examination can bring self-chastisement and can rescue the soul from a prolonged sleep in the dreadful sickness of sin. Nevertheless, only the confession of sin to the Lord God, through Jesus Christ, can bring the soul to a state of healing and eternal salvation.

By its own definition, **salvation** is a Divine work; *not* a human achievement. It is a deliverance done in and for the sinner by the Holy Spirit, which deliverance the sinner is unable to achieve on his own or for himself: *"He saved us, not on the basis of deeds which we have done in righteousness, but according to His mercy, by the washing of regeneration and renewing by the Holy Spirit."* [81]

Therefore, the New Testament clearly and repeatedly asserts that **salvation** is exclusively by the Grace of God, through faith in Jesus Christ, apart from one's own good works: *"For by grace you have been saved through faith; and that not of yourselves, it is the gift of God; not as a result of works, so that no one may boast."* [82] Another like it is this: *"For we maintain that a man is justified* [declared not guilty] *by faith apart from* [without] *works of* [obedience to] *the Law* [of God]." [83]

Accordingly, one's **repentance from sin** and one's **saving faith in Jesus Christ** are *"the gift of God,"* [84] which no man can earn for himself or for others. If you can earn salvation, it becomes your wages; it ceases to be the free gift of God. Indeed, no amount of good works can suffice to remove the sinner's guilt and spiritual stains before the Holy God! **Salvation must be received, not earned; it must be asked for, not worked for**.

Yes, indeed, both **repentance** and **faith** are granted to the **sinner** [the self-righteous is excluded from salvation] who, humbly and earnestly acknowledging his/her own spiritual bankruptcy, calls upon the Lord Jesus for salvation. They are God's two prerequisites for the sinner's salvation, and they are granted freely to the sinner, at the moment the sinner, informed and willing, calls upon the Lord Jesus Christ for his own personal salvation.

A Prayer for You: *Dear Lord, may the reader of these words be granted genuine repentance from sin and a saving faith in the Lord Jesus Christ! As he calls upon the Lord Jesus for salvation, may You grant him Your precious salvation forever! In Jesus' Name I pray. Amen!*

YOUR REGENERATION IS INSTANTANEOUS!

The moment you call upon the Lord Jesus Christ for your personal salvation, the Holy Spirit will indwell you forever! He is equally God as is the Father and as is the Son. He will **seal** you as God's eternal property, and He is given to you as a pledge, a down payment, of your eternal inheritance! [85] He is your Divine Guest, your Infallible Guide, your Supreme Teacher, your Almighty Helper, and your Loving Comforter.

Indeed, the believer in Christ, having been raised out of the death of sin, now possesses a new life of holiness,[86] of inner peace,[87] and of comforting fellowship with the Heavenly Father.[88] Therefore, yours is a new lifestyle characterized by victory [89] over sin, by your daily reliance upon the Divine strength [90] of Christ, by a genuine hunger for God's Word,[91] by a deeply rooted commitment to obey God in all aspects of life,[92] and by the blessed assurance of your current possession of eternal life.[93]

The Scriptures use the term **regeneration** to refer to the Divine Act that brings this change in your inner disposition and in your daily lifestyle. **Regeneration**, however, is **not** a gradual work done in or by the believer. To the contrary, **regeneration** is an instantaneous change performed by the Holy Spirit, at the moment the sinner receives Christ. The ***full results*** of this instantaneous change, however, will be manifested gradually in the transformed lifestyle of the new believer in the Lord Jesus Christ.

Here are **seven** clear **New Testament Illustrations** revealing the instantaneous nature of Biblical **regeneration**:

1. With a decisive act of the human will responding to God's call, the three thousand at Day of Pentecost had an instantaneous experience of the New Birth. [94]
2. By a spontaneous confession of his faith in Jesus Christ, the Ethiopian Treasurer of Queen Candace was instantly saved. [95]
3. By a simple act of his will surrendering to the Risen Christ, the persecutor of the Church, the Jewish Theologian Saul of Tarsus, was instantly transformed [96] into Paul the great Apostle of the Lord Jesus Christ.
4. The Roman Centurion Cornelius, [97] his family, and his many friends, while responding wholeheartedly to the faithful proclamation of the Word of God, had an instantaneous spiritual resurrection that carried its effects into the rest of their lives.
5. Many Greeks were instantaneously saved in Antioch.[98]
6. In the ancient City called Philippi, Lydia the saleswoman and her household experienced an instantaneous, evident, Divinely- granted spiritual resurrection described with the Bible words: *"and the Lord opened her heart."* [99]
7. A similar salvation experience was that of the Jailer of Philippi and his family who *"rejoiced greatly, having believed in God with his whole household."* [100]

Accordingly, the Holy Spirit does the eternal work of **regeneration** upon the sinner, ***instantaneously***! The results, however, will be seen gradually, throughout the life of the believer on earth, as he gradually grows onto the blameless likeness of the authentic humanity of the Lord Jesus Christ.

YOUR REGENERATION IS NON-REPETITIOUS!

therwise known in the Holy Scriptures [101] as the New Birth,[102] **regeneration** is a *once-for-all* experience in the life of the believer in Christ. It is instantaneous, non-repetitious, and irreversible. It is a sovereign act of the Holy Spirit in the repentant believing sinner, which *in a moment of time*, becomes a historical, non-repetitious, irreversible experience.

Regeneration carries its effects into the present and the future life of the new believer in the Risen Christ: *"Therefore if anyone is in Christ* [a saved person]*, he is a new creature; the old things passed away; behold, new things have come."* [103] It creates for you the permanent prospect of a new lifestyle of righteousness.

In other words, the Holy Spirit's **Act of Regeneration** is in essence laying aside *"the old self with its evil practices,"* [104] and putting on *"the new self who is being renewed to a true knowledge according to the image of the One who created him."* By **regeneration,** the Holy Spirit provides salvation from the **penalty** of sin, and installs within the believer a newly built-in **capacity** to obey and to please God, to restore the **Image of God** in the sinner.

Accordingly, once the sinner calls upon the Lord Jesus in an informed and sincere appeal for personal salvation, *the matter is settled eternally* with the Heavenly Father. It no longer will be necessary for this sinner to make another such appeal for salvation. He is already saved, eternally, forever!

In addition, note that the *calling* on the Lord Jesus specified as the step to salvation in Romans 10:13, refers to a **volitional personal choice** made independently by the sinner, not coerced by an outside agency. The original text in its original language indicates that this is a calling done by turning towards the Lord Jesus and appealing to Him for help, for personal salvation. The Greek Aorist Tense (the New Testament was originally written in ancient Koine Greek) of the verb *"will call"* indicates that the action of calling is done once for all; not to be repeated.

Therefore, once you sincerely make such a calling to the Lord Jesus Christ, the Holy Spirit performs His eternal work of **regeneration** in you. Thus, your **regeneration** is instantaneous, non-repetitious, and, as you will see later (page 40), is irreversible. It is the *beginning* of the believer's new love for God, which will be displayed to the world via the believer's new lifestyle of obedience to God's Word. Such obedience is the evidence of our love for the One who loved us to the end: *"If you love Me, you will keep* [obey] *My commandments."* [105] We will remain loyal to Him in all circumstances, at all times, and at all cost!

YOUR STEPS TO RECEIVE CHRIST THE SAVIOR & LORD

As a member of this corrupt, sinful and condemned world of humanity, for reasons known only to Him, the Lord God loved YOU so much that He sent His Son Jesus Christ to die in your place and for your salvation. Your saving faith in Him, once for all, will remove God's judgment from you, and will install eternal life within you. You, *the lost and condemned sinner*, will be transformed into **a saved sinner** seeking after God's righteousness. Carefully read the following passage from God's Word: [106]

> *For God so loved the world* [including YOU]*,*
> *That He gave His only begotten Son,*
> *That whoever believes in Him*
> *Shall not perish* [in the Lake of Fire]
> *But have eternal life.*
> *For God did not send the Son*
> *Into the world, to judge the world,*
> *But that the world might be saved through Him.*
> *He who believes in Him is not judged;*
> *He who does not believe*
> *Has been judged already,*
> *Because he has not believed*
> *In the name of the only begotten Son of God.*

Indeed, your **saving faith** in the Lord Jesus Christ will be the spiritual channel through which the Holy Spirit will transform you into a permanent member of the Family of God. This involves a Divine **YES!** It is a supernatural and once-for-all transformation of the sinner receiving

Christ. Note the *becoming* aspect of a genuine salvation: [107]
> *But as many as received Him* [Jesus Christ],
> *To them He gave the right*
> *To become* [the special] *children of God,*
> *Even to those who believe in His* [Christ's] *name,*
> *Who were born, not of blood*
> *Nor of the will of the flesh nor of the will of man,*
> *But of God.*

In summary, it is your eternity that we are talking about. The decision is entirely yours and yours alone. You can either receive Christ now, or you can reject Him. Procrastination of salvation is tantamount to a rejection of the Savior. There is no neutral grounds and the alternative to God's gift of eternal life is the well-deserved eternal torment in **Hell** after death.[108] However, your regeneration performed by the Lord God will be instantaneous, non-repetitious, and irreversible. All that the Lord God does is eternal. So will be your salvation — everlasting! The Divine Surgeon starts His saving work with your **regeneration**, He continues with your **sanctification** onto the wonderful likeness of Christ, and He will culminate it with your **glorification** into His glorious Heaven.

Therefore, possessing a Biblically informed understanding of God's simple and marvelous plan for your eternal salvation, right now and wherever you are, **take these three steps** without delay, and say an eternal **YES!** to the Lord Jesus Christ:

FIRST STEP: TAKE AN HONEST, HARD LOOK AT YOURSELF.

Do you recognize and readily confess your utterly sinful condition [not in the finite eyes of people] before **The Holy One**, **a helpless condemned sinner,** and that you are in a desperate need for the Savior?

Indeed, no church membership, no religious practices, no good works, no talents, no achievements, and no refinement can impress The Most High! The sincere and honest confession of your sinful condition is essential for your acceptance with the Lord God. Take to heart this serious warning of the Word of God: *"He who conceals his* [own] *transgressions will not prosper* [God's definition of success]*, but he who confesses and forsakes them will find compassion."* [109]

The Lord Jesus Christ accepts and receives sinners conscious of their own sinfulness; but He rejects totally those refusing to acknowledge their sinfulness, holding to their own alleged self-righteousness. However, no one is too great a sinner for our Almighty God to save past, present, and future!

Do you sincerely desire that the Lord God would turn you away from your present life of sin, from all and every one of your sins, to make you a permanent and noble slave of righteousness? If yes, take the second step:

SECOND STEP: CAREFULLY LOOK AT THE SAVIOR.

Do you recognize the Risen Christ as God Himself who appeared in human flesh? Do you wholeheartedly believe that the Lord Jesus Christ is the only Savior of the world? If so, do you sincerely believe that the Lord Jesus Christ is the sinless **God-Man** who died for your sins and rose the third day from among the dead for your salvation? Are you fully convinced that He is both willing and able to save you from the everlasting **penalty** of your sins, from the **power** of sin upon your daily life, and eventually from the **presence** of sin on earth, into the eternal glories of Heaven? If so, do you earnestly want Him to become your own personal Savior, too? Do you want Him to become the Master of your daily lifestyle? If yes to all of these questions, take the third step:

THIRD STEP: SINCERELY RECEIVE THE SAVIOR.

Given the fact of the uncertainty of human life and that man always is at the brink of eternity, one's next step may well be into another world. Therefore, it is both prudent and urgent that your eternal destiny and your relationship to God would be settled right now and at this place, once for all. Accordingly, right now, and wherever you are, sincerely and earnestly ask the Lord Jesus Christ to become your own personal Savior and Lord of life. One of His precious promises that cannot be broken is this: *"for WHOEVER WILL CALL ON THE NAME OF THE LORD* [Jesus Christ] *WILL BE SAVED."* [110] YOU MUST TRUST HIS WORD, FOR HE IS GOD WHO NEVER TOLD A LIE.

If you indeed come to the Lord Jesus just as you are, in all sincerity asking for your eternal personal salvation, He will receive you to Himself; He certainly will **not** cast you out: *"the one who comes to Me I will certainly not cast out."* [111] Here is a sample prayer you may want to use right away and wherever you are:

Lord Jesus Christ,

Thank you for coming to earth and dying for my personal salvation. I sincerely confess to You my lost sinful condition, which calls for Your righteous judgment upon me. Often I have disobeyed Your Precious Word and frequently I have broken Your Perfect Laws. Helplessly, I am deeply enslaved to sin. Therefore, I know that I deserve Your just condemnation of me to everlasting punishment in the Lake of Fire. However, now and in this place, I come to You accepting Your death and resurrection on my behalf and for my benefit, as my own Substitute. I ask You, as You have promised in Your Word, to become my personal Savior and Lord of my daily life. I ask You to turn me away from my life of sin, enabling me to make generous restitution to all against whom I have sinned, forgiving all my sins, making me a new creature in Christ, giving me the new birth into the Family of God, and granting me eternal life. I also ask You to help me from now on to live the Christian life pleasing to You. I thank You for answering this my sincere and earnest prayer, by saving me at this moment and in this place. Amen!

My Signature _____

Sign this prayer, and keep the following information in a safe place, for your future reference: Following my reading of **What Must I Do to Be Saved?**, I sincerely and earnestly received the Lord Jesus Christ as my personal Savior and Lord of my life.

Day I Received the Lord Jesus _____ At _____ am / pm

Date ____ Month _____ Year _____

Place _____

"And all things you ask in prayer, believing, you will receive."
Matthew 21:22

THE ASSURANCE OF YOUR SALVATION

After you sincerely and earnestly complete such prayer, rest assured by God's infallible Word that **NOW** you have become a member of the special household of God! **NOW** all your sins are forgiven! **NOW** you possess eternal life! Indeed, once you have prayed this prayer sincerely and earnestly, you have become a born-again Christian, a special child of God on your way to the glories of **Heaven**! This blessed assurance is based exclusively on the precious promises of God's Word; **not** *on the way you feel* right now or later: *"For you are all sons of God through faith in Christ Jesus."* [112] Go ahead, shout out loud and clear: Glory and praise to my Savior Jesus Christ!

Trust His Word; His promises never fail! Here is another of His precious promises: *"I WILL PUT MY LAWS UPON THEIR HEART, AND ON THEIR MIND I WILL WRITE THEM, He then says, AND THEIR SINS AND THEIR LAWLESS DEEDS I WILL REMEMBER NO MORE."* [113] **MOST CERTAINLY, THE LORD JESUS HAS ACCEPTED YOUR PRAYER AND HAS RECEIVED YOU ONTO HIMSELF, FORGIVING ALL YOUR SINS!** [114] HALLELUJAH! Thank you Lord!

Therefore, from now on, whenever you pray to your Heavenly Father, you must *"draw near with a sincere heart in full assurance of faith."* [115] Indeed, your Heavenly Father does **not** lie, does **not** deceive, and does **not** bluff! Accordingly, *"these things I have written to you who believe in the name of the Son of God, so that you may know* [with absolute certainty] *that you have eternal life."* [116]

Indeed, our failures declare us human, and our humanity

indicts us weak and sinful; but the sanctifying Grace of God sufficiently enables the believer in Christ — granting victory over sin and temptation, beyond all human frailty: *"For it is God who is at work in you, both to will and to work for His good pleasure."* [117] However, when we, the weak and struggling believers in Christ, do fall in sin, *"If we confess our sins, He is faithful and righteous to forgive us our sins and to cleanse us from all unrighteousness."* [118] Treasuring His Word in our hearts will help keep us from falling in temptations to sin. Memorize His Word!

While *no sin* can cause you to lose your eternal salvation granted to you by the Lord, your **prompt daily confessions of your sins** to the Lord are necessary for the continuation of uninterrupted fellowship with the Father,[119] for receiving answers to your prayers,[120] for your own spiritual growth and maturity, and for your usefulness in the Kingdom of God. ***Unconfessed sin*** can kill your appetite for the Word of God, can hinder your prayers, [121] can diminish your love for the brethren, [122] can weaken your efforts to bring souls to Christ, can blemish your testimony for Christ, can ruin your personal reputation, and can create doubts in your mind about your own salvation. There is no wisdom in holding to your sin, regardless of your feelings and your circumstances! *It is always wise and prudent to confess it and to forsake it promptly.*

Furthermore, the saved sinner, in addition to the newly acquired divine nature, continues to possess the old human nature which entices him to sin. [123] He continues to live in a sinful world abundant with temptations to sin.[124] In addition, Satan and his demons wage spiritual wars against the believer in Christ, seeking to devour him back into ungodliness. [125] Thus, the believer at times is apt to fall into, though not to remain in, sin. [126]

Naturally, falling in certain sin or sins will generate thoughts of doubts about one's own salvation. However, the confession of your sins is the means to eradicate such doubts. Indeed, the confession of your sins directly to the Lord will rejuvenate your desire to study the Word of God and to do the Will of God. Nevertheless, a life of righteousness generally is the inevitable fruit of a genuine experience of salvation. [127] The more your life morally resembles that of your glorious Savior, the stronger your **assurance of salvation** [128] will become.

Accordingly, for the follower of Jesus Christ, the state of the soul following physical death is no longer "the unknown." The Lord Jesus Christ has assured us of **eternal life**, in no uncertain terms.

Similarly, that state after death is not one "in doubt" to the believer in Christ; for the Holy Scriptures constitute the most solid grounds for the **assurance of our salvation**: *"This is the promise which He Himself made to us: eternal life."* [129] Blessed assurance: the Lord Jesus is mine, and I am His! To doubt your own salvation is equivalent to doubting the truthfulness of God's Word, and to questioning the reliability of God's precious promises. These doubts will grieve the Holy Spirit indwelling you. However, your study and memorization of God's Word will help you drive away such doubts. NOW and FOREVER, you are a saved person on your way to the glories of **Heaven**! [130]

CONFESS YOUR FAITH IN JESUS CHRIST PUBLICLY!

0 ahead; frequently and boldly tell the whole world about your wonderful and glorious Savior, and about your newly-found magnificent salvation! Here is our Lord's clear instruction on this vital point of confessing Him before men: [131]

Therefore everyone who confesses
Me before men,
I will also confess him
Before My Father who is in heaven.
But whoever denies Me before men,
I will also deny him
Before My Father who is in heaven.

Actually, you confess or you deny Christ by your words, by your silence, by your actions, and by your inactions.[132] Indeed, through your hourly choices on the side of righteousness, your daily clean speech, [133] your constructive attitudes, your transparently wholesome conduct, [134] and your sacrificial efforts to spread the Word of God around the world (Mat. 28:18-20), through all of these together, **the Lord Jesus Christ and His moral glory** increasingly will become visible to those around you, particularly to those who knew you prior to your regeneration. [135]

   Certainly, genuine Christian living will open up for you various opportunities to proclaim your Savior to many who need His saving words and His saving grace. Speak out the oracles of God in no uncertain terms, without apology, and in a candid and loving manner becoming of a faithful *ambassador* of Jesus Christ. [136]

The Niagara Falls in Western New York
Speak of the majesty of their Creator

> *"Sing to the LORD, bless His name;*
> *Proclaim good tidings of His salvation*
> *from day to day."*   Psalms 96:2

Via your daily prayers, and by the study and memorization of God's Word, [137] the Holy Spirit will guide you to what your Heavenly Father wants you to do for His good pleasure. [138] Obey Him in every point, wholeheartedly! Indeed, as you obey the truths [139] you learn each day, the indwelling Holy Spirit will introduce you to additional truths for your daily obedience. He wants to use you, your natural talents, your spiritual gifts, your time, and your financial resources, to spread the whole counsel of God faithfully and powerfully, as a good and triumphant soldier of Jesus Christ.

However, keep in mind that not all around you will appreciate your conversion to the Lord Jesus Christ. This, because your life gradually will become a walking sermon, and some folks simply do not like sermons. Therefore, learn to be patient with and gentle [140] toward those who exhibit their resentment toward your new lifestyle. Pray for them, perhaps in time they will experience this same magnificent salvation which you now possess. However, do not neglect to tell them about your Savior: ***"for with the heart a person believes, resulting in righteousness, and with the mouth he confesses, resulting in salvation."*** [141] For one person, this author would love to hear from YOU about your recent salvation experience! Let me know that you did receive the Lord Jesus following your reading of **What Must I Do to be Saved?**

Accordingly, My Friend, ***"Let us hold fast the confession of our hope without wavering, for He who promised is faithful."*** [142] Never apologize for doing what is pleasing to the Lord God! Daily remind yourself that you were joined to the Risen Jesus Christ in order that you ***"might bear fruit for God."*** [143] This required fruit is that the Lord Jesus, the Hope of Glory, would become visible in your life to those who know you.

YOU MUST BE BORN AGAIN!

THE HOLY SPIRIT NOW BEGINS HIS WORK OF SANCTIFICATION!

Purity of thought, purity of emotions, purity of speech, and purity of conduct — all are your Heavenly Father's holy objectives for your new lifestyle.[144] *"Keep yourself free from sin"* [145] is the admonition from Paul the Apostle to young Timothy. It is your Heavenly Father's desire to purify you from all sin, in preparation for that gloriously blessed meeting with your Savior — face-to-face! Therefore, daily you should ask the Heavenly Father to *"cleanse your conscience from dead works to serve the living God."* [146]

However, to judge everything in this world by mere material standards, is to be subject to the desires of the sinful human nature within. This demonic pattern of thinking dominant in our days will drive you to live a life dominated by the senses, apart from faith in the Lord Jesus Christ. Watch yourself closely; beware of **materialism**!

Yes, indeed, to be gluttonous in food; to be effeminate in luxury; to be slavish in pleasure; to be lustful and lax in morals; to be selfish in use of one's possessions; and / or to be extravagant in the gratification of material desires — is to live in total disregard to the Word of God and to the very existence of God Himself. Such materialistic living is theologically known as *practical atheism*. Our Lord reminded us that we cannot serve two masters, God and **materialism**: *"No one can serve two masters; for either he will hate the one and love the other, or he will be devoted to one and despise the other. You cannot serve God and wealth."* [147]

Nevertheless, immediately following your earnest prayer for salvation, the Holy Spirit will begin to transform you, to mold you onto the grandeur moral likeness of your Savior. Through the process of **sanctification**, the Holy Spirit works to actualize in the life of the believer the righteousness of Jesus Christ imputed to him at moment of regeneration. The desired outcome is that you *"may be holy both in body and spirit."* [148] This Divine Process, beginning with the *Act of Regeneration*, is called in Scripture the process of **sanctification**. It begins at the moment you receive Christ, and it continues to the moment you meet Him face to face in Heaven. Thus, **sanctification** is the progressive development of the new love for God acquired at your moment of *regeneration*. Indeed, the degree of our love for God is evidenced by the degree of our obedience to God: *"By this we know that we have come to know Him, if we keep His commandments."* [149] **DO NOT RESIST THE HOLY SPIRIT INDWELLING YOU!**

Therefore, utilizing the written Word of God, prayer, and other experiences of life, the Holy Spirit daily will perform on you His beautifying moral work of **sanctification**. [150] Your *only* Model of *authentic humanity* is none other than the Lord Jesus Christ Himself, as He is revealed clearly on the pages of the infallible Scriptures. The effectiveness of the Holy Spirit's work of **sanctification** upon you is determined by the degree of your understanding of and your obedience to the Holy Scriptures. A Baptist pastor insightfully wrote in a published article: **"To know God truthfully, to understand the Scripture comprehensively, and to live life rightly is the greatest conceivable human blessing."**

In sanctifying you, the Holy Spirit seeks to produce in your daily life the Christ-like **Fruit of the Spirit.** Here are the most noble and highly esteemed nine specific components of His Fruit: [151]

> *But the fruit of the Spirit is love, joy,*
> *Peace, patience, kindness, goodness,*
> *Faithfulness, gentleness, self-control;*
> *Against such things there is no law.*

By **sanctification**, the Holy Spirit provides salvation from the **power** of sin over your daily life, preparing you daily for Heaven's eternity. He progressively replaces your old sinful ways with new righteous ways. He takes away the ungodly and He installs the godly. He dims your view of the perishing earthly, and He brightens your view of the permanent heavenly. The temporal and the sensual gradually fade away into the background, while the eternal moves to the forefront of your daily living and giving: *"For the grace of God has appeared, bringing salvation to all men, instructing us to deny ungodliness and worldly desires and to live sensibly, righteously and godly in the present age, looking for the blessed hope and the appearing of the glory of our great God and Savior, Christ Jesus, who gave Himself for us to* *redeem us from every lawless deed, and to purify for Himself a people for His own possession, zealous for good deeds."* [152] **It is always a rewarding experience to do the Will of God.** However, it is always a bitter experience to move against the revealed Will of God. Your Will be done, O Lord our God, Your Will be done!

Repeatedly remind yourself that because now you are a true child of God, you do not face temptations alone. [153] Indeed, your Heavenly Father will not allow you to be tempted with that more than you can bear. [154] As you saturate your mind with the written Word of God, the Holy Spirit will cleanse you from sin. [155] Through unwavering faith in your Savior, you are promised complete victory over the temptations of the world. [156] This faith is nourished and developed by the studying and the hearing of the Word of God, [157] by its application to life, accompanied with earnest and frequent prayers.

In addition, use the Word of God to tell Satan off. Continually say "No!" to the old nature within you, and always say "Yes!" to the prompting of the Holy Spirit. Learn to distinguish His inner voice from that of your adversary & that of your own old nature. Here is one tip: the Holy Spirit will never prompt you to disobey God's will revealed in the Bible; such prompting is definitely NOT from God! Divine Guidance is never self-contradictory; it is always in harmony with the Holy Scriptures. Whatever the Bible actually teaches is indeed God's Will for your life, at all times and under all circumstances. However, youthful lusts should be handled only in one way [158] — **run away from them**! Christian manhood is measured not by the indulgence in sin, but by your victories over temptations, your obedience to the Word of God.

Keep in mind that the infallible Bible will drive you away from sin; [159] but if you allow it, sin will drive you away from the Holy Bible. Never allow sin to defeat you! Forsaking all sin, and implementing the righteousness of Christ into your daily lifestyle, would transform you daily into a child of God mirroring the moral glory of your Savior.

Furthermore, meditate on the things listed in Philippians 4:8. Occupy yourself doing what is right in God's sight, so that you will have no time to do what is wrong in God's sight.

Frequently ask your Heavenly Father to fill you with His Truth and His Love, and with all sincerity.

Moreover, the believer is commanded to put on ***the whole armor of God.*** [160] The armor is the Lord Jesus Himself and the pieces of the armor are the graces of Christ: the girdle of truth, the breastplate of righteousness, the shoe of the Gospel of Peace, the shield of faith, the helmet of the hope of salvation, the sword of the Spirit, and the practice of prayer. You would do well to study this New Testament passage early on (Ephesians 6:10-20), learning how to put on ***the whole armor of God***.

Finally, in addition to reading and studying the Bible, you must embark on reading quality Christian publications. These will enhance your understanding of the Holy Scriptures, and will provide you with wisdom that comes only from above. Learn the many great hymns and spiritual songs of the Christian Faith. They will help you sing joyfully onto the Lord and they will assist you in keeping your mind on heavenly matters. Many of them proved themselves a source of encouragement and comfort to me. I have no doubt that you likewise will find them a blessing to you as well.

YOUR REGENERATION IS IRREVERSIBLE!

Once the Holy Spirit does His marvelous work of regeneration on you, you are saved forever! No one, not even you, can remove you from the blessed hand of your Savior: *"My sheep hear My voice, and I know them, and they follow Me; and I give eternal life to them, and they will never perish; and no one will snatch them out of My hand. My Father, who has given them to Me, is greater than all; and no one is able to snatch them out of the Father's hand. I and the Father are one."* [161] As a regenerated person, you belong to the Lord Jesus Christ, the King of kings and the Lord of lords. From this moment of regeneration and forward, you are one of His sheep, **you are royalty forever!** No one can change you back into a goat, no one can remove you from the Family of God, and no one can rob you of this your eternal position in the Lord Jesus Christ!

In addition, by receiving the Lord Jesus Christ, you are born into the special Family of God; and you never can be unborn: *"**But as many as received Him, to them He gave the right to become children of God,*** *even to those who believe in His name, who were born, not of blood nor of the will of the flesh nor of the will of man, but of God.*" [162] No one can undo the new birth generated by the Lord God. You are a child of God forever possessing the heavenly Father's righteous nature (1 Peter 1:3; 13-16), which new lifestyle will display characteristics of God's righteousness. A genuine child of God possesses an irrevocable built-in guard against habitual sinning: "*No one who is born of God practices sin, because His seed abides in him; and he cannot* [practice] *sin because he is born of God.*" [163] God's seed of righteousness *abides* in the believer — remains permanently, cannot be reversed. Therefore, once a child of God, you always will remain a child of God.

Furthermore, the moment you receive the Lord Jesus, the Holy Spirit plants within you the precious seed of eternal life. Indeed, the everlasting life of God is imparted to the believer at his moment of regeneration: "*He who believes in the Son* [of God] *has* [already possesses] *eternal life.*" [164] The born-again believer in Christ will never come to judgment before God: "*Truly, truly, I say to you, he who hears My word, and believes Him who sent Me, has eternal life, and does not come to judgment, but has passed out of death into life.*" [165] He will never perish in eternal torment: see "*they will never perish*" quoted above.

Moreover, a genuinely born-again believer is predestined [set his eternal destiny] by the Lord God to become conformed to the image of God's Son: "*For those whom He foreknew, He also predestined to become conformed to the image of His Son.*" [166] God's sovereign predestination cannot be revoked, cannot be modified, and cannot be reversed. The born-again believer will surely and ultimately become like the Lord Jesus Christ: "*We know that when He appears, we will be like Him, because we will see Him just as He is.*" [167]

Accordingly, your regeneration is irreversible! Once truly saved, you will always remain a saved person! Those who have been forgiven their sins, reconciled to God, regenerated, converted, justified, united with Christ, sanctified, sealed by the Holy Spirit, adopted, predestined, indwelt by the Holy Spirit, and labeled The Elect of God, shall neither totally nor finally fall away from the state of Grace; but are kept by the preserving power of the Lord God.

THE BIBLE EVIDENCE OF A GENUINE SALVATION

The Bible repeatedly and clearly asserts that a genuine experience of salvation produces many significant changes in the individual's worldview and lifestyle. Among other results is the following six-fold evidence of a genuine salvation experience:

1. **A new lifestyle of habitual victory over temptations to sin.**

    The regenerated person, although he may fall in sin, he now leads a new lifestyle of righteousness: *"No one who is born of God practices sin, because His seed abides in him; and he cannot* [practice] *sin, because he is born of God. By this the children of God and the children of the devil are obvious: anyone who does not practice righteousness is not of God, nor the one who does not love his brother."* (1 John 3:9-10; cf. 5:18). He possesses a built-in capacity (his faith, a gift from God) for victory over various temptations advanced by the world of sin: *"For whatever is born of God overcomes the world; and this is the victory that has overcome the world — our faith."* (1 John 5:4).

2. **The born-again Christian exhibits new attitudes of genuine love.**
    a. He possesses a growing love toward God (1 John 4:19; 5:2);
    b. He habitually loves other born-again Christians (1John 5:1);
    c. He deals in love with his personal enemies (Matt. 5:44);
    d. He seeks the salvation of lost souls (2 Corinthians 5:14).

3. **The regenerated person acts on his faith in God's promises.**
    a. He believes that God will provide for his needs (Matthew 7:11; cf. Luke 11:13; Philippians 4:19);
    b. He believes that God will reveal His Will to him (I Corinthians 2:10-12; Ephesians 1:9);
    c. He believes that he is a fellow-heir with Jesus Christ (Romans 8:17; cf. John 5:24).
    d. He believes that whatever the Bible says is so (Psalms 19:7-8; John 20:31; 2 Tim. 3:16-17; 1 Pet. 1:21-22).

4. **The saved person has a built-in capacity to understand the Bible.**
    a. He has a growing desire for the Word of God (I Peter 2:2);
    b. The indwelling Holy Spirit gives him the ability to understand the Bible (1Corinthians 2:12-13).
    c. He adheres to sound Bible doctrines (John 8:31-32).

5. The born-again Christian possesses the ability to please the Lord God.
    a. He is predestined to do works pleasing to the Lord God (Eph. 2:10);
    b. He is exhorted to maintain an undistracted devotion to the Lord (1 Corinthians 7:35).

6. He is given, in the experience of the New Birth, the solid foundation for the assurance of personal salvation.
    a. He has the assurance of the forgiveness of his own sins (Colossians 2:13-15; I John 2:12);
    b. He has the assurance of his possession of eternal life (1 John 5:10-12; cf. John 3:16, 36; 5:24).

As the birds feed their newly born, so does the Lord God provide His spiritual food to all who are regenerated by the Holy Spirit.

    The growing presence of this six-fold evidence in one's new lifestyle speaks of a genuine salvation experience that indeed has occurred in the life of the individual. This individual is a true born-again Christian. In the midst of all your circumstances, always remember that you are a child of God! Similarly, the absence of this evidence indicates the absence of salvation. This individual MUST be born again (see: John 3:7).

FOLLOW THE LORD JESUS IN BELIEVER'S BAPTISM!

Now that you are a legitimate member of the Household of God, you must remain cognizant of the fact that your Heavenly Father has a long list of "good works" that He has planned for YOU to perform during the remaining time [hopefully, many more years] of your life on earth: *"For we are His workmanship, created in Christ Jesus for good works, which God prepared beforehand so that we would walk in them."* [168]

By obeying each of His commandments, you will learn to love the righteousness that your Heavenly Father loves, and to abhor the evil which He abhors. This learning process will cause your personality to blossom progressively and soundly in the fragrant likeness of our Lord Jesus: *"But now having been freed from sin and enslaved to God, you derive your benefit, resulting in sanctification, and the outcome, eternal life."* [169]

Accordingly, your first major step of obedience to the Heavenly Father must be that you follow Him [170] in submitting to the Christ-given **Ordinance of Water Baptism**.[171] As it was in the Early Church days that *"the Lord was adding to their number day by day those who were being saved,"* [172] so it must be in our times.

An Ancient Baptismal Pool

This addition to the membership of the local church was performed by administering the **Ordinance of Water Baptism**, to all who received Christ as Savior and Lord: *"So then, those who had received his word were baptized; and that day there were added about three thousand souls."* [173]

Therefore, you must follow the Lord Jesus by getting baptized into the membership of a New Testament local church. The blessed **Ordinance of Water Baptism** is administered by the authority of the local church, by immersion into water, [174] and in the name [175] of the Father and the Son and the Holy Spirit. It is to be administered exclusively to those who have experienced the New Birth, by receiving [176] the Lord Jesus.

By your submission to Biblical **Water Baptism**, you proclaim officially your faith in Jesus Christ, and you confess publicly your personal determination to follow Him for the rest of your life: *"For all of you who were baptized into Christ have clothed yourselves with Christ."* [177] Being immersed into water is a picture of your death with Christ to the old life of sin; and being brought out of the water is a picture of your resurrection with Christ to a new life of righteousness. Delaying this obedience to God is tantamount to disobedience.

JOIN
A NEW TESTAMENT CHURCH
IMMEDIATELY!

The elect Church of Jesus Christ is embodied physically in local churches the Holy Spirit, using godly men, has planted and is planting around the world. Thus, the local church, being the Body of Christ, is the organized company of regenerated people, baptized into water, called out to assemble themselves together in a given locality, and have covenanted themselves together to carry out the commandments of Christ.

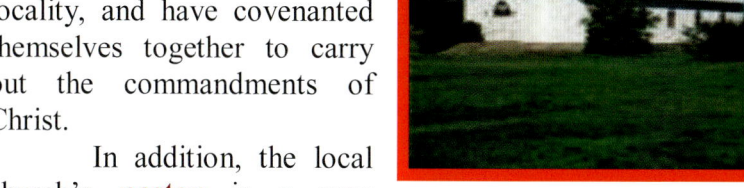

In addition, the local church's **pastor** is a man transparently leading a life pleasing to the Lord God, above reproach, and exhibiting the Fruit of the Spirit.[178] The pastorate is limited in God's Word to such a man who is *the husband of one wife*.[179] Women are assigned a different role in the local church, assigned by the Lord God Himself.[180] A man full of the Word of God [181] and prayer, [182] submissive to the written Word of God, [183] diligent in bringing souls to Christ, [184] persevering in discipling the believers in Christ, [185] and whose family lives in godliness, [186] is the pastor from God. Similar requirements for local church **deacons** are specified in 1 Timothy 3:8-13.

Likewise, today's **New Testament Church** is a local church whose teachings, [187] whose mission, [188] whose organizational structure, whose policies, and whose operational activities are completely and fully founded upon the New Testament model for the local church; and all are thoroughly in harmony with the teachings of the New Testament.[189]

Indeed, the local church is **the instrument** through which the Holy Spirit accomplishes His purposes in the world, manifests God's moral glory to the world, and exhibits the wisdom and the grace of God to the world. [190] Inevitably, then, the local church's **doctrinal** [191] and **moral** [192] **purity** is an absolute New Testament requirement. To ignore or to dilute this Biblical demand is to betray the Lord Jesus Christ. This **purity** is achieved and is maintained by the teaching of *sound doctrine*, [193] by *exhortation to godly living*, [194] and by the *exercise of church discipline*. [195] The natural outcome of such **purity** is the church's **unity** bonded with genuine *Christian love*.[196]

Clearly, a local church which openly and unapologetically expects obedience to the Christian Holy Scriptures from every one of its members *without partiality*, [197] and which proclaims boldly **the whole counsel of God** [198] revealed in Scripture — is the New Testament church you want to join via **Water Baptism**. It must be a church which consistently in all its functions adheres to excellence [199] apart from mediocrity, pursues spirituality [200] against carnality, elevates character above talent, emphasizes quality over quantity, and highly favors self-denial [201] against showmanship. Be sure that you go to a church where you solemnly join in worshiping God; not to a theater named "church" where you simply get entertained. [202]

Contemporary music — being deeply and profoundly associated with concepts, attitudes and philosophies displeasing to the Lord God — must be shunned by the believer in Christ, and must not be allowed in the local church. This is one of the criteria, a clue which you can detect early on while searching for a New Testament church. A church which uses country music, jazz, metal, rock, alternative, progressive, blues, rap, "gospel music" or the so-called "Contemporary Christian Music" (CCM), is **not** the church you want to join!

Likewise, the lustful **modern dance** is intrinsically associated with immodesty, jealousy, envy, drinking, rape, adultery, fornication, divorce, and at times even with murder. Thus, *a church that utilizes dancing* in its worship services or as a church activity is a cancerous church, off limits for the Christian desiring to please the Lord God. **You do not belong there!**

Furthermore, a New Testament church is one that seeks to **please the Lord God**, [203] not the contemporary culture, in all that it teaches and in all that it does. Such a church, though difficult to find, is necessary for your spiritual growth and for your opportunities to carry out the commandments of Christ. However, once you find such a New Testament church in your area, join it wholeheartedly, and joyfully participate in its New Testament ministries.

As you listen to the preaching and the teaching of the church, follow the good example of the believers of the ancient city of Berea who *"were more noble-minded than those in Thessalonica, for they received the word with great eagerness, examining the Scriptures daily to see whether these things were so."* [204] Compare what you hear with the actual teachings of the Bible.

Like you, the members of the church are saved sinners wrestling against sin. They have their various weaknesses as well as their strengths. While they possess many good qualities you will admire, **your only infallible Example to follow is the Lord Jesus Christ Himself**. Keep your eyes fixed upon Him, and *"through love serve one another."* [205] In addition, we are commanded: *"bear one another's burdens,"* [206] and *"while we have opportunity, let us do good to all people, and especially to those who are of the household of the faith."* [207]

YOUR REQUIRED CHRISTIAN GIVING

It is God's will for you that here, in the local church, you must learn to develop within you **the self-giving love of Christ**. Giving of your natural talents, your spiritual gifts, your time, your efforts, and your material resources is well-pleasing to your Heavenly Father. In addition to giving one-tenth [208] of your income to support the local church ministering to you and your family, you also should give, as the Lord prospers you, for the training of Christian leaders, for the mass production and distribution of quality Christian literature, for the faithful broadcasting of the Word of God, and for New Testament missionary works, both domestic and foreign. Therefore, maintain healthy finances.

While giving to charity is required, the ***foremost priority*** in your giving should go for the Gospel of Jesus Christ: ***"Do not work for the food which perishes, but for the food which endures to eternal life, which the Son of Man will give to you, for on Him the Father, God, has set His seal."*** [209] This, because ***"It is written, 'MAN SHALL NOT LIVE ON BREAD ALONE, BUT ON EVERY WORD THAT PROCEEDS OUT OF THE MOUTH OF GOD.'"*** [210] Indeed, while humanitarian giving in the Name of Christ is required (see Galatians 6:10) of the Christian, most of your giving must go toward ministering the Word of God to others (Luke 12:13-34 & John 4:13, 14). This may include, among other things, your purchase and distribution of quality Christian literature, your giving to support faithful missionaries, your giving to the training of ministers of the Word of God, and your volunteer efforts in the activities of a Christian Ministry faithful to the Word of God.

To present yourself ***"a living and holy sacrifice"*** [211] to God and His work is the New Testament admonition: ***"Therefore if you have been raised up with Christ, keep seeking the things above, where Christ is, seated at the right hand of God. Set your mind on the things above, not on the things that are on earth."*** [212]

However, if no such New Testament church exists in your area, you must seek with others in your area to organize a New Testament church pleasing to the Lord God. This author and my organization are available to offer guidance and assistance for planting a New Testament church in your area. Our Lord assured us that His sheep, having been granted eternal life, will follow the Good Shepherd: *"My sheep hear My voice, and I know them, and they follow Me; and I give eternal life to them, and they will never perish; and no one will snatch them out of My hand."* [213]   Follow Him!

CONSIDER THIS VITAL TRUTH

The Lord Jesus Christ assured us that a man's life requires more than mere material things. We need **spiritual nourishment**, the food that came down from Heaven: *"Man shall not live on bread alone, but on every word that proceeds out of the mouth of God."* (Matthew 4:4). Indeed, the Lord God has created mankind in such a unique manner that **physical nourishment**, the material food, sustains the **physical dimension** of the person; and that **spiritual nourishment**, the written Word of God (the Bible), sustains the **spiritual dimension** of the person. Its infallible truths can transform the believer's life forever.

Therefore, a person (including YOU) can suffer seriously from *spiritual malnutrition*, just as he (YOU) can suffer from *physical malnutrition*. **Do not allow it to happen to you! Feed on the Word of God day and night** (read Psalms 1), and invest time and energy in earnest prayers. The Bible commands us to live in an unceasing condition of prayer, of devotion and of obedience to God.

As the Lord God has made us dependent on physical nourishment, He likewise made us dependent on spiritual nourishment

I Am Available To Assist You

Indeed, the Lord God has forgiven all your sins, the so-called small ones and the big ones, and He has granted you eternal life, for the sake of the Lord Jesus Christ! The Holy Spirit has come in to indwell you forever as your Divine Guest. He is here, among other things, to strengthen you in times of weakness, to comfort you when you need encouragement and comfort, to rebuke you for sins committed, to warn you against temptations you will face, and to guide you into doing God's Will, for the rest of your life. Hallelujah, you are NOW saved by the Grace of God, through faith in the Lord Jesus Christ!

Consequently, as a new child of God, **now** you need Biblical instruction on the **assurance of your personal salvation**, on how to proceed from here, on how to overcome temptation, how to live the Christian Life specified in the Holy Scriptures, how to feed daily on the Word of God, and how to serve the Lord God in this evil world.

I have written a series of twelve instructional and informative letters to help you on these lines. They are *free of charge*, no strings attached, and they will come to you simply for the asking, as the Lord enables me to do so. Please use the enclosed **Feedback/Order Form** to request them. If the Form is missing, send me a letter.

In addition to these, I would be delighted to give you Biblical guidance and instruction along each and all of Biblical matters related to faith and practice. I have founded **The Biblical Counseling Center™** for this specific purpose: I offer genuine Biblical counseling, solid Bible teaching, consultation, and selected Christian literature, including my own writings.

Moreover, I hold Bible Studies in the Monroe County Area, New York, to which I invite and welcome YOU. Call my office for up-to-date information. I also teach the Bible on Facebook and on my Websites. I am confident that you, as others did, will find these Bible studies thoroughly Biblical, refreshingly encouraging, joyfully strengthening, deeply inspirational and widely informative — quite relevant to your daily lifestyle! Do not forget to send me the enclosed **Feedback/Order Form**.

Whatever you do, keep in mind that YOU need spiritual assistance right away. Today is better than tomorrow, and this week's start is urged upon you. Please feel free to contact me at any time. I am fully committed to serve you and your family with joy:

Dr. Habib J. Khoury, Th.D.

Email: DrKhoury@bamius.org
Phone: (585) 586-9191
Fax: (585) 586-2755
Mail: P. O. Box 485 Fairport, New York 14450-0485
Official Website: www.bamius.org
Biblical Counseling Website: www.bamicounseling.org

"The righteous man will flourish like the palm tree; He will grow like a cedar in Lebanon." Psalms 92:12.

A Palm Tree with Fruit   A Cedar Tree in Lebanon

Use this Booklet as a Tool for Evangelism

Partner with us in spreading this salvation booklet into many homes. We would offer you a discount of nearly 30% on each carton of 24 copies you order directly from this publisher. We would also pay for the shipping to any address in the U.S. or Canada. **You are free to give them away and/or to sell them for some extra income**. *For you, this is 24 copies of* **What Must I Do to Be Saved**? *delivered at your doorsteps, for only* **USD $168**. *You can place as many orders as you want and for as many cartons as you want. This will cost you only* **USD $168 per carton, delivered to your address in the U.S.A. or Canada** *(New York State delivery addresses, please add 8% sales tax, a total of* **$181.44** *per carton)*. **This is a standing offer, ending on December 31, 2012.** *Call us (585-586-9191) or fax us (585-586-2755) for any questions regarding this offer. We will ship within 24 hours of receipt of your paid order.*

To order, specify how many cartons you want (one or more than one), include your check or money order for the full amount payable to **BAMI Publications**, *give us the delivery address, and mail together to:*

BAMI Publications / Evangelism
P. O. Box 485
Fairport, New York 14450-0485

To Whom to Give *What Must I Do to Be Saved?*

1. Your family, friends and neighbors
2. Your church staff & congregation
3. High school & college students & graduates
4. Your teachers, physicians, dentists & attorneys
5. Your public officials
6. Media editors, anchors, reporters
7. Those you meet while shopping
8. Anyone who would read it

Do not delay, send your order today!

References Made In the Text

[1] Quoted from Acts 16:30, in the NT.
[2] **Philippi** was the first town in Macedonia where the Apostle Paul established a church, to which he later wrote the *Epistle to the Philippians*.
[3] Quoted from Acts 16:31, in the NT.
[4] Quoted from Psalms 18:30, in the OT.   Emphasis mine.
[5] See Mark 2:17, in the NT.
[6] See Luke 19:10, in the NT. A **lost person** is one who is wasted or allowed to spoil, as to his usefulness to God's purposes in the world, as revealed in the Holy Scriptures. Also, a **lost person** is an unsaved person condemned to eternal damnation in the Lake of Fire. He becomes a **saved person** through his experience of the New Birth. For a well-documented Biblical understanding of the New Birth, read: Dr. Habib J. Khoury, **The New Birth**.
[7] Compare Matthew 8:22; John 5:25 and Ephesians 2:1, in the NT.
[8] Quoted from Romans 3:23, in the NT.
[9] Read Ecclesiastes 7:20, in the OT.
[10] See: Romans 3:10, 23, in the NT.
[11] Read: Ephesians 2:3; 4:18, in the NT.
[12] See: Ephesians 4:18; Colossians 1:21, in the NT.
[13] Read Jeremiah 17:9, in the OT.
[14] See Romans 8:7, 8, in the NT.
[15] Read Ephesians 2:2, in the NT.
[16] See 2 Corinthians 4:7, in the NT,
[17] Read Titus 3:3, in the NT.
[18] See Romans 6:17, in the NT.
[19] Quoted from Psalms 12:1, in the OT.
[20] See Psalms 73:22, in the OT.
[21] Read Isaiah 53:1, in the OT.
[22] Quoted from Isaiah 59:11, in the OT.
[23] Quoted from Isaiah 59:2, in the OT.
[24] Quoted from Luke 16:15, in the NT.
[25] Quoted from Proverbs 10:29, in the OT.
[26] Quoted from Romans 6:23, in the NT.
[27] Quoted from Ecclesiastes 3:15, in the OT.
[28] Quoted from Hebrews 9:27, in the NT.
[29] Quoted from Galatians 6:7, in the NT.
[30] Quoted from John 3:3, in the NT.   Emphasis mine.
[85] Quoted from II Corinthians 13:5, in the New Testament.
[86] Quoted from Psalms 26:2, in the Old Testament.
[33] See Matthew 5:48, in the NT.
[34] See: Galatians 1:6-10 & Titus 3:10, 11, in the New Testament.
[35] Read: I Corinthians 5:1-13; cf. II Corinthians 12:20, 21 & Ephesians 5:11-21, in the New Testament.
[36] Quoted from Matthew 5:48, in the NT.
[37] See John 5:14; 8:11, in the NT.
[38] Read: Galatians 6:1; James 5:16, in the NT.

[39] See: II Samuel 19:19; II Chronicles 6:37; James 3:6.
[40] Read: Isaiah 1:2; Job 34:37; Romans 4:5; 5:6.
[41] See: Joshua 7:1; Matthew 23:14.
[42] Read: Leviticus 4:13, 22, 27; James 4:17.
[43] See: Romans 7:15-17, in the NT.
[44] Read: Romans 8:7; I John 1:8; Jeremiah 13:23.
[45] The judicial act of God in regard to **sin** is judgment (Matthew 11:22, 24; II Peter 2:4, 9), accusation (Jude 9), damnation (Matthew 23:33; Mark 3:29), and condemnation (John 3:19; 5:24). God's verdict of the sinfulness of every human being is based on: **1) Inherited Sin**, the sin nature transmitted mediately by natural generation from parent to child (Psalms 51:5; John 3:6); this sin automatically generates the *spiritual death* of the person, at the moment of conception in the womb; **2) Imputed Sin**, Adam's first sin imputed to the entire human race, all having participated in the first sin while in germ form in Adam (Genesis 3; Romans 5:12); this sin brings *physical death* to every man; and **3) Personal Sin**, the sins committed by the individual; this sin breaks man's fellowship with God and calls upon His acts of chastisement (I John 1:5; 2:11; Hebrews 12:1-13). Should sinful man die without the Savior, he will go to *everlasting torment*. In the New Testament Book of Revelation, this is labeled *"the second death."*
[46] Quoted from Romans 6:23, in the NT.
[47] Quoted from Psalms 119:4, in the OT.
[48] Quoted from John 14:15, in the NT.
[49] Quoted from Matthew 22:37, in the NT; cf. Deuteronomy 6:5; 10:12; 30:6, in the OT.
[50] Quoted from John 3:36.
[51] **The Christian Bible** (both OT & NT) is of **dual authorship**: the Lord God is the sovereign Author, and chosen instruments of God were the sanctified human writers. Utilizing their individuality, personal interests, literary styles, and life experiences, the Holy Spirit *breathed out* of the human writers *the words* of the original texts in their original languages. Thus, never a true prophet spoke out of his own initiative. Therefore, the words of the Bible are the words of God and the voice of Scripture is the Voice of God. Conclusively, *whatever the Bible says is so*. Read: II Timothy 3:16, 17 and II Peter 1:19-21, in the NT. The Lord God expects the Christian to conform his daily life to the dictates and the principles of the infallible Scriptures. For a clear overview, an informative introduction to, and a variety of methods to study the Bible, read: Dr. Habib J. Khoury, **So You Are New to the Bible**.
[52] Quoted from Ezekiel 33:11, in the OT.
[53] Quoted from I Timothy 2:3, 4, in the NT.
[54] The Greek verb translated **believe**, is always rendered in the Active Voice when referring to the sinner's act of faith in the Lord Jesus. This indicates that this faith is volitional on part of the sinner, not coerced by an outside agency, Divine or otherwise. **Faith** is distinguished repeatedly from *human merits*. See: Romans 4:3-6; Galatians 2:16; Ephesians 2:8, 9, in the NT.
[55] Quoted from Luke 24:47, in the NT.
[56] Quoted from John 3:15; cf. I John 5:13, in the NT.
[57] Read: II Peter 3:9, in the NT.
[58] See: John 3:16-18, in the NT.
[59] Quoted from Mark 1:15, in the NT.
[60] Quoted from Acts 26:20, in the NT.
[61] See: Luke 13:3; Acts 3:19; 17:30; cf. Luke 17:3, in the NT.
[62] Read: Hebrews 11:6; cf. Romans 1:17; 14:23, in the NT.

[63] Quoted from John 3:18, in the NT. Emphasis mine.
[64] Quoted from II Corinthians 7:10, in the NT.
[65] Read: Psalms 51:1, 2 in the OT, & II Corinthians 7:9, 10 in the NT.
[66] Read his story in Luke 19:1-10, in the NT.
[67] Quoted from Luke 19:8, in the NT.
[68] Quoted from Luke 19:9-10, in the NT.
[69] Quoted from Ecclesiastes 3:15, in the OT.
[70] Quoted from Acts 3:19, in the NT.
[71] The Greek New Testament verb *epistrephō*, to **turn** or to **convert**, is one of the major theological terms in the NT. The great thrust of John the Baptist's ministry was to turn men to God (Luke 1:16-17). Although the word may refer to a simple bodily movement (as in Mark 5:30), there is a powerful moral theme that runs through the Book of Acts, emphasizing repentance from sin: **1)** The Apostle Peter preached that men should repent and be converted [turned], so that their sins might be blotted out (Acts 3:19); **2)** The healing of Aeneas caused many people to turn to the Lord (Acts 9:35); **3)** Many in Antioch heard the witness and turned to the Lord (Acts 11:21); **4)** The Apostle Paul preached that pagans should turn to the living God (Acts 14:15); **5)** The Jerusalem Council recognized that Gentiles had turned to God (Acts 15:19); **6)** The Apostle Paul was commissioned to turn men from darkness to light and from the power of Satan to God (Acts 26:18); and, **7)** Paul did preach that both Jews and Gentiles (non-Jews) should repent and turn to God (Acts 26:20). The New Testament Epistles continue this strong theme of repentance from sin, as the Apostle James urges believers to convert the sinner from the error of his way (James 5:19-20). Conclusively, without repentance from sin, there is no forgiveness of sins. Adapted from Dr. Stewart Custer, **Witness for Christ: A Commentary on the Book of Acts.**
[72] Quoted from James 2:19, in the NT.
[73] Quoted from Luke 18:17; cf. Matthew 18:3 in the NT.
[74] See: Romans 6:17, 18.
[75] Quoted from Romans 5:1, in the NT.
[76] Quoted from Acts 4:12, in the NT.
[77] Quoted from I Timothy 3:16, in the NT.
[78] Quoted from Habakkuk 1:13, in the OT.
[79] Quoted from Isaiah 59:2, in the OT.
[80] Quoted from John 6:44, in the NT.
[81] Quoted from Titus 3:5, in the NT.
[82] Quoted from Ephesians 2:8-9, in the NT.
[83] Quoted from Romans 3:28, in the NT. Emphasis mine.
[84] Quoted from Ephesians 2:8, in the NT.
[85] See: Ephesians 1:13, 14, in the NT.
[86] Read: Colossians 3:1-17, in the NT.
[87] See: John 14:27; 17:13, in the NT.
[88] Read: John 4:23, 24; 14:12-14, in the NT.
[89] See: John 7:38, in the NT.
[90] Always claim Philippians 4:13, in the NT.
[91] Read: I Peter 2:2 & Colossians 3:16, in the NT.
[92] Read: Romans 6:15-23; cf. Acts 5:29 & I John 2:5, in the NT.
[93] Memorize: John 3:16, 36, in the NT.
[94] Read: Acts 2:41-47, in the NT.
[95] See: Acts 8:26-40, in the NT.

[96] Read: Acts 9:1-22, in the NT.
[97] Read: Acts 10:1-11:18, in the NT.
[98] See: Acts 11:20-24, in the NT.
[99] Read: Acts 16:14, 15, in the NT.
[100] See: Acts 16:25-34, in the NT.
[101] Read our Lord's teaching on the **New Birth** in John 3:1-21, in the NT.
[102] For a detailed study of the Bible's teachings on *Sin* and *The New Birth*, read: Dr. Habib J. Khoury, **Urgent Letter to My Niece**.
[103] Quoted from II Corinthians 5:17, in the NT.
[104] Read: Colossians 3:9, 10, in the NT.
[105] Quoted from John 14:15; cf. I John 5:3, in the NT.
[106] Quoted from John 3:16-18, in the NT. Emphasis mine.
[107] Quoted from John 1:12-13, un the NT. Emphases mine.
[108] The Holy Scriptures speak of **Hell** after death as a real and everlasting place of torment. This is the **Lake of Fire** originally prepared for Satan and his demons (Matthew 25:51), and has become the final abode of the lost sinners (Matthew 25:46). It is a place of damnation and judgment (Matthew 23:33), from which there is no escape. Death, Hades, Satan, demons and lost sinners will be cast into the **Lake of Fire** for their everlasting destiny (Revelation 20:14, 15). In Matthew 18:8, 9; 25:41 both *"Hell fire"* and *"the everlasting fire"* speak of the same place that lost sinners will *"be cast into."* The New Testament phrase *"the everlasting fire"* is a translation of the Greek phrase "**To pur to aiōnion**," which denotes that the tormenting fire is without end. Therefore, the **Lake of Fire and Brimstone** is an everlasting place of unquenchable fire, of *"disgrace and everlasting contempt"* (Daniel 12:2), and of miserable *"weeping and gnashing of teeth"* (Matthew 8:12). It is a place described as a lake of fire and brimstone, where *"their worm does not die"* (Mark 9:48). It is a furnace of fire, an everlasting fire, an outer darkness, a bottomless pit, and a place of everlasting punishment. God's justice demands such an everlasting place and punishment for every sinner unrepentant from sin and rejecting the Savior. This description of the eternal state of *"the wicked"* sounds like an everlasting state of awfully painful burning, of constant worm activity, added to a continuous, tormenting feeling of falling away into outer darkness.
[109] Quoted from Proverbs 28:13, in the OT. Emphases mine.
[110] Quoted from Romans 10:13, in the NT. Emphasis mine.
[111] Quoted from John 6:37, in the NT.
[112] Quoted from Galatians 3:26, in the NT.
[113] Quoted from Hebrews 10:16, 17, in the NT.
[114] Read: I John 5:9-12, in the NT.
[115] Quoted from Hebrews 10:22, in the NT.
[116] Quoted from I John 5:13, in the NT. Emphasis mine.
[117] Quoted from Philippians 2:13, in the NT.
[118] Quoted from I John 1:9, in the NT.
[119] See: I John 1:6, in the NT.
[120] Read: I John 3:22, in the NT.
[121] See: Psalms 66:16-20, in the OT.
[122] Read: I John 3:14-24, in the NT.
[123] See: Romans 7:14-25, in the NT.
[124] Read: I John 2:15-17, in the NT.
[125] See: II Corinthians 11:14 & I Peter 5:8, 9, in the NT.
[126] Read: I John 3:7-10, in the NT.

[127] See: I John 2:29, in the NT.
[128] For a detailed and well-documented study of the Bible's teaching on the believer's assurance of salvation, read: Dr. Habib J. Khoury, **The Assurance of Our Salvation**, published by **BAMI Publications**™.
[129] Quoted from I John 2:25, in the NT.
[130] According to the Bible, those saved by the Grace of God through faith in Jesus Christ, at the translation of the Church, will be transformed into perfect Christ likeness, and will have everlasting life with Christ, in the personal presence of God. The Scriptures repeatedly speak of a literal place named **Heaven**. It portrays **Heaven** as the place of God's Throne, surrounded by countless hosts of angels, Seraphim, Cherubim and other heavenly creatures. Its human occupants are *"only those whose names are written in the Lamb's book of life"* (Revelation 21:27). With the permanent personal presence of the Lord God and the Lamb, there is no need of the sun or of the moon in **Heaven**, *"for the glory of God has illuminated it, and its lamp is the Lamb."* (Revelation 21:23). Wonderfully, *"In the daytime (for there will be no night there) its gates will never be closed"* (Revelation 21:25). Indeed, **Heaven** is the glorious presence *"with the Lord."* Compared to our world at its possible best, **Heaven** is a *"very much better"* eternity *"with Christ"* (Philippians 1:23). It is a permanent place of manifested glory for those who placed their saving trust in Christ. For the believer in the Lord Jesus Christ, **Heaven** is a place of everlasting *"rest,"* of joy, of service, and of worship. In **Heaven**, our eyes *"will see the King in His beauty"* (Isaiah 33:17). Our bodies will be distinguished eternally as *"imperishable,"* raised in *"glory"* and *"power"* (1 Corinthians 15:43). In **Heaven**, our knowledge and our understanding will reach perfection. *"And He will wipe away every tear from their eyes; there will no longer be any death; there will no longer be any mourning, or crying, or pain; the first things have passed away"* (Revelation 21:4). *"And nothing unclean, and no one who practices abomination and lying, shall ever come into it"* (Revelation 21:27). **Heaven** is the place of eternal holiness, for the curse of sin *"shall be no more."* The distressed Prophet Job described the effects of **Heaven**'s holiness upon its human population: *"There the wicked cease from raging, and there the weary are at rest. The prisoners are at ease together; they do not hear the voice of the taskmaster. The small and the great are there, and the slave is free from his master"* (Job 3:17-19). In **Heaven**, no poverty, no bankruptcy, no hunger, and no homelessness would exist, for all the redeemed people of God will *"become rich"* (2 Corinthians 8:9). Accordingly, **Heaven** is the eternal residence of every believer in the Lord Jesus Christ. Christ's Resurrection has made it possible and has guaranteed the glorious hope for the believer in Christ *"to be absent from the body and to be at home with the Lord"* (2 Corinthians 5:8).
[131] Quoted from Matthew 10:32, 33, in the NT.
[132] See: Titus 1:16, in the NT.
[133] See: Colossians 4:6, in the NT.
[134] Read: Colossians 3:1-25, in the NT.
[135] Read: II Corinthians 6:3-10; cf. Galatians 2:20, in the NT.
[136] Read: II Corinthians 5:17-21.
[137] Memorize: Psalms 1:1-6, in the OT.
[138] See: I Peter 1:12-16, in the NT.
[139] Read: I Peter 1:22-25, in the NT.
[140] Read: II Timothy 2:25, in the NT.
[141] Quoted from Romans 10:10, in the NT.
[142] Quoted from Hebrews 10:23, in the NT.

[143] Quoted from Romans 7:4; cf. Galatians 5:22, in the NT.
[144] See: I Timothy 4:12, in the NT.
[145] Quoted from I Timothy 5:22, in the NT.
[146] Quoted from Hebrews 9:14, in the NT.
[147] Quoted from Matthew 6:24, in the NT.
[148] Quoted from I Corinthians 7:34, in the NT.
[149] Quoted from I John 2:3, in the NT.
[150] Read: Romans 6:6-23, in the NT.
[151] Quoted from Galatians 5:22-23, in the NT.
[152] Quoted from Titus 2:11-14, in the NT.
[153] Read: Philippians 4:13, in the NT.
[154] See: I Corinthians 10:13, in the NT.
[155] See: John 17:17 in the NT & Psalms 119:9-11 in the OT.
[156] Read: I John 5:4, in the NT.
[157] Read: Romans 10:17 & II Timothy 3:14-17, in the NT.
[158] See: II Timothy 2:22, in the NT.
[159] Memorize: Psalms 119:9-16, in the OT.
[160] Read: Ephesians 6:10-18, in the NT.
[161] Quoted from John 10:27-30, in the NT.
[162] Quoted from John 1:12-13, in the NT.
[163] Quoted from I John 3:9, in the NT.
[164] Quoted from John 3:36, in the NT.
[165] Quoted from John 5:24, in the NT.
[166] Quoted from Romans 8:29, in the NT.
[167] Quoted from I John 3:2, in the NT.
[168] Quoted from Ephesians 2:10, in the NT.
[169] Quoted from Romans 6:22, in the NT.
[170] The Lord Jesus Himself was baptized leaving us an example to follow. See: Mark 1:9-13, in the NT.
[171] The ordinance of Water Baptism was given by the Lord Jesus to His Church (Matthew 28:18-20).
[172] Quoted from Acts 2:47, in the NT.
[173] Quoted from Acts 2:41, in the NT.
[174] See: Acts 8:38, 39, in the NT. Note the phrases *"went down into the water"* and *"came up out of the water."* **This indicates the Apostles practiced immersion in water, and so must we.**
[175] Read: Matthew 28:19, in the NT.
[176] See: Romans 6:3-5, in the NT.
[177] Quoted from Galatians 3:27, in the NT.
[178] See the God-given requirements for the **pastoral office** in I Timothy 3:1-7 and Titus 1:5-9, in the NT.
[179] The Biblical requirement *"the husband of one wife"* indicates that the **office of a pastor** is exclusively for men. Also, the repeated use of the masculine pronoun in reference to the pastor demands a man to occupy the office; not a woman. Therefore, we must conclude that the heresy of a woman pastor is not from God. Women preachers are imposters, in a state of defiance to God. They are **not** God's servants. See: I Timothy 3:2; cf. Titus 1:6, in the NT.
[180] In the local church, the woman is **not** allowed by God *"to teach or exercise authority over a man"* (I Timothy 2:12). This Bible teaching is based on the facts of the original

creation and the fall of the First Parents (I Timothy 2:13, 14), and is **not** rooted in the peculiarities of any culture past or present. All of the 12 apostles of the Lord Jesus were men; **no woman** was included. Compare: I Corinthians 14:34-37; Titus 2:5; Ephesians 5:22; I Peter 3:1; and Colossians 3:18.

[181] See: II Timothy 2:15; 4:1, 2; cf. I Timothy 5:17, 18 and Colossians 3:16, in the NT.
[182] See: I Thessalonians 5:17; Ephesians 6:18-20, in the NT.
[183] Read: I Timothy 4:6-16, in the NT.
[184] See: II Timothy 4:5, in the NT.
[185] Read: II Timothy 2:1, 2; cf. 1:13, 14, in the NT.
[186] Read: I Timothy 3:1-5, in the NT.
[187] Read: Galatians 1:6-10, in the NT.
[188] See: Matthew 28:18-20, in the NT.
[189] For a summary of the major teachings of the Bible, read: Dr. Habib J. Khoury, **Our Christian Faith,** published by **BAMI Publications**™. Or, see online: www.bamius.org/statements.html.
[190] Read: Colossians 1:24-28, in the NT.
[191] See: Galatians 1:6-10 & Titus 3:10, 11, in the NT.
[192] Read: I Corinthians 5:1-13; cf. II Corinthians 12:20, 21& Ephesians 5:11, in the NT.
[193] Read: Ephesians 4:14, 15; I Timothy 1:3, 10; 4:6, 13 & 16; 6:1-5; II Timothy 4:1-4; Titus 1:9; 2:1, 7; & II John 9, 10, in the NT.
[194] Read: I Thessalonians 4:1; II Thessalonians 3:12; I Timothy 2:1-4; II Timothy 4:2; Titus 2:6, 9, &15; Hebrews 3:13; I Peter 5:1; Jude 3, in the NT.
[195] Read: Romans 16:17; I Corinthians 5:4-11; I Thessalonians 5:14; &II Thessalonians 3:6, 14, in the NT.
[196] Read: Ephesians 4:13-16 & Colossians 3:14, in the NT.
[197] See: II Thessalonians 3:6 & James 2:1-9, in the NT.
[198] Read: II Timothy 4:1, 2, in the NT.
[199] Read: Romans 2:18; Philippians 1:10, in the NT.
[200] Read: Colossians 1:9-14; cf. Galatians 5:16, 24-26;& Philippians 3:19, in the NT.
[201] See: Luke 9:23-26; cf. Galatians 2:20, in the NT.
[202] See: II Timothy 4:1-8, in the NT.
[203] See: I Thessalonians 2:4 & Galatians 1:10; cf. I John 3:22 & I Corinthians 7:23.
[204] Quoted from Acts 17:11, in the NT.
[205] Quoted from Galatians 5:13, in the NT.
[206] Quoted from Galatians 6:2, in the NT.
[207] Quoted from Galatians 6:10, in the NT.
[208] See: Malachi 3:8-10, in the OT.
[209] Quoted from John 6:27; cf. Luke 12:13-34 & John 4:13, 14, in the NT.
[210] Quoted from Matthew 4:4 in the NT; cf. Deuteronomy 8:3 in the OT.
[211] Read: Romans 12:1-21, in the NT.
[212] Quoted from Colossians 3:1, 2; cf. Matthew 16:23 & Philippians 3:17-21, in the NT.
[213] Quoted from John 10:27, 28, in the NT.